Board Basics

By Warren Tapp

Published in Australia by Sid Harta Books & Print Pty Ltd,
ABN: 34632585293
23 Stirling Crescent, Glen Waverley, Victoria 3150 Australia
Telephone: +61 3 9560 9920, Facsimile: +61 3 9545 1742
E-mail: author@sidharta.com.au

First published in Australia 2023
This edition published 2023
Copyright © Warren Tapp 2023

Cover design, typesetting: WorkingType (www.workingtype.com.au)

ISBN: 978-1-922958-15-0

ii

About the Author

Warren Tapp is a Fellow of the Australian Institute of Company Directors and was a facilitator of their Company Directors Course for 10 years. He's been a director on 26 boards and the chair of 13. He has also been on advisory boards and many board committees.

He founded his own company to provide consulting advice to boards on corporate governance and other processes and has been a keynote speaker at conferences in Australia and overseas on this topic. He has also published *So You Want to Be a Company Director,* which is available on his website store at www.tappadvisory.com.au, alongside a selection of videos and other resources on boards, governance and general business.

His qualifications include a Master of Business Administration and a Master of Law. He also has a

Graduate Diploma in Applied Corporate Governance and has completed the Advanced Company Directors course. Warren is currently completing a doctoral thesis in law on the topic of governance.

Warren lives on the Gold Coast in Queensland, Australia.

Introduction

first saw the need for this book after I was invited to speak to a group of postgraduate students about corporate governance at a university business school. Realising that many of these students would either end up in roles reporting to boards or perhaps even become board members themselves, it was clear to me they had no knowledge or understanding of how a board of directors operates. I also realised there were probably many other people who don't understand the basics of a boardroom and that it might be useful for those currently in an executive role, or those seeking a new career direction, to develop their understanding. The aim of this book is not to be a technical guide but rather a simple introduction to the role and responsibilities of a board of directors. I've also added a chapter about how to get on a board, which complements my previous book, *So, You Want to be a Company Director.*

I have also included a chapter on what to look out for before you join a board so that you open a can of worms before it's too late. I hope this book is helpful to you and that you learn something about the basics of a board of directors. While the book is primarily based on the Australian corporate environment, most of the fundamentals still apply wherever you are in the world. Enjoy the book!

Warren Tapp

Contents

Chapter 1:
The History of Boards

The concept of a board of directors dates as far back as the 1600s to England when the Dutch East India Company and other such entities were established, and the shareholders realised they needed people to represent them and oversee the management of the company. In most countries today we have a unitary board. That is one board governing the company. However, in some countries in Europe, they often have two boards: one made up of management and union representatives; the other a senior board comprised of experienced businesspeople.

Australian Corporations law has historically borrowed heavily from British company law. Its legal structure now consists of a single national statute called the *Corporations Act 2001*. This statute is administered by a single national regulatory authority: the Australian Securities and Investments Commission (ASIC). Since provisions of the act can be traced back to pioneer legislation in the United Kingdom, references are frequently made to British court judgements. Though other forms are permitted, the main corporate forms in Australia are public and private (or proprietary) companies, both of which predominantly have limited liability. This means the liability of the shareholders is limited to the extent of their share capital. The liability of the directors, however, is absolutely unlimited.

Upon Federation in 1901, the Constitution of Australia granted limited powers to the Australian parliament in relation to corporations, but each state had a residual power in relation to anything not within the Commonwealth power. As it was mostly the concern of each separate state legislature, there were significant differences in legislation between the states. After the Second World War, it became increasingly clear the legislative differences between the states were creating unnecessary costs for companies that operated beyond one state, so the Commonwealth and the states formed a uniform national companies code in 1962. The problem with this scheme was it did not provide for uniformity in amendments of the legislation or changes of government or policy in each state. To overcome the defects of the first scheme, a second cooperative scheme was agreed upon in 1978 and implemented by 1982. All laws and amendments were then to be agreed upon by a ministerial council and automatically applied in each jurisdiction. This second scheme led to the creation of the National Companies and Securities Commission, the forerunner to what we have today in ASIC.

While an improvement on the first scheme, the 1982 scheme still presented significant difficulties — mainly due to the National Companies and Securities Commission delegating administrative functions to various state commissions, while still retaining control of takeovers and policy. The Commonwealth then sought to take sole responsibility for Corporations law in Australia. In 2001, the current arrangement was created, and the states referred their power with respect to corporations entirely to the Commonwealth through the creation of the *Corporations Act 2001*.

Australian companies are incorporated by

registration with ASIC. An application for registration specifies whether the company is to be proprietary or public and the type of liability for the shareholders of the company. Shareholder liability can be either unlimited with share capital, limited by shares, limited by guarantee, or no liability (when the company's sole objects are mining or mining-related activities). The most common form of business entity in Australia is a company limited by shares. Proprietary companies must include the word Proprietary or Pty after their name, are not allowed to raise capital on public equity markets and cannot have more than 50 shareholders. Only companies publicly listed on the Australian Securities Exchange (ASX) can engage in public fundraising activities, although crowdfunding more recently has opened up another means for a company to raise capital.

Companies incorporated overseas that wish to conduct business in Australia must either incorporate a wholly or partly owned subsidiary company in Australia or register a branch office in Australia. Australian companies can be fully foreign owned, though they must have an office address in Australia and one director needs to reside in Australia.

Proprietary companies often are used for private ventures or as subsidiaries of public companies, including foreign companies. Other proprietary companies might simply be a shell company set up to limit the owner's liabilities for other business structures such as trusts or partnerships.

If a foreign company chooses to establish a branch office in Australia, it must be registered as a foreign company under the *Corporations Act 2001*. Such registration does not create a separate legal entity; rather, it creates a public record and registration of a foreign company's presence in Australia. Upon registration, ASIC will issue the company with a certificate of incorporation and an Australian Company Number (ACN), which must be quoted on all correspondence and invoices issued by the company. For a branch office of a foreign company, it will be issued an Australian Registered Body Number (ARBN), which is similar to an Australian Business Number (ABN). If the company wants to trade, it will also need a Tax File Number and an ABN.

Australian companies must have share capital. The minimum number of shareholders for both a proprietary and public company that is limited by shares is one. There is no upper limit on the number of shares that can be issued. How the company deals with that shared capital is strictly regulated by the *Corporations Act 2001*. By default, shareholders have one vote per share. Corporations listed on the ASX cannot deviate from the one-share, one-vote rule. Directors must convene a meeting if members with more than 5 per cent of voting rights request so in writing, stating the resolution they wish to be put. The *Corporations Act 2001* also gives the general meeting the power to alter or amend the company constitution when a minimum vote of 75 per cent is achieved. A shareholder does not have a right to receive a dividend; however, once a final dividend is declared, it becomes a debt payable by the company to the shareholder from the date stipulated for payment.

Corporate governance standards are not just a matter of comply and explain. They have been taken into account by Australian courts when determining the scope of a director's duties. The ASX Corporate Governance Council's best practice recommendations state that the chief executive officer and the chair of the board should be separate people. This is not necessary for a private or family-owned company. The

ASX recommendations also state the board of directors should have a majority of independent directors, and that the chair also should be independent. Directors are considered independent if they are not executives, employees or shareholders of the company. These guidelines also state the company should have a remuneration committee, chaired by an independent director, with at least three members — most of whom should be independent. A publicly listed company should also have an audit committee of at least three members with an independent majority, chaired by an independent director who is not the chair of the board.

The way to recognise the structure of a company is by the words following the company name. Pty and then Ltd indicate it is a proprietary or private company only. If the company name appears only as Ltd, this indicates it's a public company; however, this doesn't identify if it is listed on the ASX or simply a public company that is unlisted. The term Ltd is also used after the name of a company that is limited by guarantee. These types of organisations mainly operate in the not-for-profit sector.

Every company will have a constitution. This could be a standard template that you can download from the

ASIC website, and if it's not changed from the template, it can be adopted by the shareholders of the company. The shareholders might wish to make amendments to the constitution to suit the purposes of that particular company. This can be done only by a majority rule. A constitution is simply a contract between the directors and the shareholders as to how the company will operate.

The laws in Australia are very rigid in allowing for the removal of directors by a simple majority vote in an ordinary resolution. For public companies there must be a meeting with two months' notice, with the director sought for removal having the right to be heard. For private companies that do not offer shares to the public and have fewer than 50 shareholders, this rule can be replaced with a different rule that might involve a simpler procedure. The removal of a director from office does not affect their claim for possible breach of contract. Directors of Australian companies must be a natural person and be at least 18 years old. They do not have to be Australian citizens or have any particular qualification or experience, but other legislation might impose restrictions and qualification requirements for some companies.

An undischarged bankrupt cannot be a director, but they might be an employee of the company, and ASIC maintains a list of persons who've been banned from acting as a director. A person might be appointed as a nominee director by a shareholder, and that person is expected to act in the interest of the person who appointed them. This can be a problem for some people as the law says a director owes their duty to the company to which they have been appointed. A private or proprietary company must have at least one director who might also be the company secretary and sole shareholder, though there is no requirement for a private company to have a company secretary. A private company must have at least one director who resides in Australia. A public company must have at least three directors, of whom at least two must reside in Australia, and it must have at least one company secretary who resides here.

In the event of a vacancy on the board, a "replaceable rule" allows the board of directors to appoint other directors; however, they must be confirmed at a general meeting of shareholders. A director's remuneration for a publicly listed company is determined by the board itself. The directors pay themselves the amount they decide from a shareholder-approved maximum pool, with shareholders having a non-binding say on remuneration. If at two consecutive general meetings of shareholders, the result is that more than 25 per cent of shareholders vote against the directors' remuneration, all directors must stand for election again within 90 days. A director who receives remuneration or other benefits from a company is treated (for accounting and tax purposes) as an employee of the company.

If a company in Australia attempts a takeover of another company, it should be noted that takeovers are regulated directly by very technical rules in the *Corporations Act 2001*. Corporate transactions and any restructuring might also be subject to anti-monopoly or foreign investment rules — as well as employment protection and special industry protection legislation. The Takeovers Panel, which is operated by ASIC, oversees any such takeovers in Australia.

So, as you can see, while the history of boards dates back hundreds of years, in Australia and similar countries the structure and operation of boards is in a mature stage with well-defined legislation, regulations and practices.

Chapter 2:
Legal Structures

have outlined the different legal structures that have a board of directors, but to summarise again, a private or proprietary limited company can have just one director and one shareholder, and an unlisted public company needs to have a minimum of 15 shareholders and at least two directors. A publicly listed company on the Australian Securities Exchange (ASX) must have at least three directors, two of whom are resident in Australia. Previously, I also mentioned the corporate structure of a company limited by guarantee, but I want to clarify this further. Usually, a not-for-profit company will have a board of directors, and the guarantee indicates that instead of shareholders they have members. The liability of each member is guaranteed only to the extent of a nominal amount, often only $1 or $2.

If a company limited by guarantee becomes insolvent, the members are protected to the extent of that small amount. A director's liability remains unlimited. These types of companies are used mainly for not-for-profit organisations, as any profits they make cannot be distributed to the members but must remain within the company as part of working capital. The extent to which the liability of a director is unlimited indicates just how seriously the law takes the role of a director in participating in decisions related to the company and the shareholders' benefit. The *Corporations Act 2001* has extensive sections regarding a director's duties.

Australian directors are subject to similar duties found in other jurisdictions, particularly the duty of loyalty and the duty of care. All directors have a duty to act in the best interest of the company; this is primarily identified as being for the benefit of shareholders. Surveys suggest that Australian directors, more so than their counterparts in other countries, view their primary obligation as to create shareholder value. However, in recent times, a trend has emerged with directors also having obligations to other stakeholders. These might include suppliers, employees and the wider community. As a result, many boards in Australia are adopting policies in relation to corporate and social responsibility that indicate the board is aware of its obligations to other stakeholders — while retaining its primary responsibility or duty to the company and its shareholders.

Directors have the duty to strictly avoid conflicts of interest. When a director has any interest in a transaction, they must give full disclosure and avoid participating in that decision. For example, a director who is on the board of two different companies (with conflicting interests), must not only declare that interest, they also must give full disclosure on the potential harm to the other company. When a director wishes to take an opportunity in which the corporation might possibly have an interest, they must gain the fully informed consent of the whole board. The law also states that a director must not act in a way to gain a personal interest; nor can they gain any benefit by disclosing any confidential information shared with them as part of their role as a director of the company. A director is required to act honestly and in good faith at all times. The other part of the law indicates they must act with a duty of care; that is, they cannot be negligent in their role in a way that will result in damage to the company or the shareholders' interests.

The *Corporations Act 2001* also includes a business judgement rule, which states if a director acted honestly and in good faith when making a business decision that unfortunately resulted in losses or to detriment to the company and its shareholders, they will not be held liable. This means when a director takes appropriate steps to inform themselves about the subject matter of a judgement — and they reasonably believe their decisions to be appropriate — they will not be held liable. However, this also means a director cannot ignore any warning signs or reports that indicate there is a risk of potential harm or damage to the company. They also cannot delegate these responsibilities to management or other people. One of the prime responsibilities of a board of directors is to avoid insolvency — the situation when a company is unable to pay its debts when they fall due. Worse still is allowing the company to trade while knowing it's insolvent. If a director is — or should be reasonably aware — that a company is likely to become insolvent and does nothing about it, the director is liable to pay compensation.

Depending on the industry the company operates in, there are several pieces of legislation other than the *Corporations Act 2001* which a board of directors should be familiar with. Some of these include:

- Employment law

- Taxation law

- Superannuation law

- Environmental law

- Intellectual property law

- Trade practices law

- Industry-specific regulations

From all this, you can see a board and its directors need to have access to good legal advice to ensure the company is complying with a wide range of legislation. Quite often a company will have an in-house lawyer providing advice to the board — or perhaps the company secretary will have legal qualifications, so they can provide this advice. If this is not the case, a board usually will use outside legal advisors to assist in ensuring compliance.

Before we finish on legal matters, I want to mention one other legal structure that is outside the *Corporations Act 2001*. Each state in Australia has its own legislation allowing people to establish what is called an incorporated association. For example, in Queensland, the *Incorporated Associations Act 1981* regulates the establishment and operation of these bodies. These entities do not have a board of directors but rather a management committee. An incorporated association must have a minimum of seven members and a minimum of three people on the management committee. This must include a chair (or president), a secretary and a treasurer. These all operate on a not-for-profit basis, which means any profits must be retained within the association for the benefit of the entity and cannot be paid out to the members. Each state has agencies that monitor and control incorporated associations, such as Consumer Affairs and the Office of Fair Trading. There appears to be a lesser level of liability for members of the management committee of an incorporated association, but there are financial penalties depending on what breaches of the particular act have occurred. I suggest that if you are or become a member of a management committee you should still adhere to the same principles as a director of a company and act in accordance with the rules of the *Corporations Act 2001* regarding a director's duties, even though they might not apply.

An association also might be unincorporated. This means it is simply a gathering of people with a common interest without a corporate entity or a separate body in the same way as an incorporated association. Such a gathering of people cannot form contracts as one body; nor can they open bank accounts, except in the name of one of the members. There is also no protection for the members, and should an unincorporated association run into legal problems, all of the members will be subject to the liability that might occur as a result. This is the reason a lot of people with a common interest form incorporated associations, as the entity itself is allowed to form contracts, borrow money and open bank accounts, while maintaining a high degree of protection for the members of the association.

If you are ever invited to join a board of directors,

you will be required to sign a consent form that you are doing so willingly, and you'll be entered on the register of directors for that company with ASIC. Your liability begins from the time your registration is recorded. If you wish to resign from a board of directors you should give your resignation in writing to the chair (and perhaps the company secretary). Ask them to forward your resignation to ASIC so you are removed from the register as a director. I've always found it best to contact ASIC afterwards to check if your name has been removed; otherwise, your liability might continue even after you've left.

Today, companies have amendments to their constitution that allow directors to access information up to seven years after they have left the board should they have to defend themselves in a matter that occurred while they were on the board. Previously, directors would normally sign a Deed of Access, which allowed for the same right to access information should legal action be taken against them during the seven years after their departure from the board. It is important to ensure that you are protected even after you have left a board of directors. Most companies have liability insurance that covers the directors, senior management and officers for any legal expenses that occur in the wake of any claims against them. I suggest any future director should carefully read such a policy to see what it covers and what exclusions it might have so they know what amount of protection they each have.

Chapter 3:
Role of a Director

There are many different types of directors. You might find one day that you become a non-executive director. This means you are simply a board member with no executive or operational responsibility within the company. You might find yourself as an independent director — meaning you have no previous or current connection to the company in any way, including as a shareholder or former employee. If you end up as an executive director this means you not only sit on the board, but you work day-to-day in the company itself. For example, a managing director is a member of the board and is often the chief executive of the company.

A nominee director is someone appointed by one

of the major shareholders to represent their interests on the board. A nominee director not only has the responsibility of ensuring they look after the interests of the shareholder who appointed them, they must also act in the best interest of the company, including all the other shareholders. One might occasionally hear about "shadow" directors. These are people who are not legally members of the board but exert great influence from behind the scenes. And, in fact, they can be seen by the courts to have been a director without having legally or formally done so.

The role of the chair of the board is to chair the meetings when the board convenes, and they have no additional powers beyond that of any other director. They tend to be paid more than the other directors as their workload is generally larger. Often, they will be required to have regular meetings with the chief executive or other staff, and they might be required to represent the board and the company at functions. The chair is also responsible for working with the company secretary to plan the agenda for the forthcoming board meeting and to approve the minutes of the previous one. The chair is also expected to mentor the other directors, monitoring their professional development and behaviour.

Quite often a board will have committees. Some might include:

- Remunerations Committee

- Audit Committee

- Finance Committee

- Risk Committee

- Governance Committee

- Strategy Committee

I've often seen boards with committees that I regard as operational, such as a human resources or marketing committee. In my opinion, these are not required as there is potential for the board to become too involved in operational matters. A board should definitely have a remuneration committee that has the responsibility of nominating future directors and senior executives and their remuneration. It should have an audit committee to deal with the internal and external auditors for the company, as well as a risk committee that reviews and minimises the company's risks.

A board can create any committee it wishes to, and it can operate on either a permanent or short-term basis. Generally, most committee members will be board members, one of whom will chair the committee. It's quite appropriate to invite other people who are not members of the board to sit on a committee if they bring particular skills or expertise that strengthens the effectiveness of the committee. It should be noted that committees must not be allowed to make decisions on behalf of the board; they should only make recommendations. The purpose of a committee is to spend more time focussing on a particular issue so the whole board does not have to deal with the minutiae. This allows the board to simply make decisions based on the detailed recommendations of the committee.

Minutes should be kept of all board meetings, recording who was there and what decisions were made. The minutes should include the times the meeting started and finished, as well as any times that directors left the room or returned. The company should keep these minutes on file, and in my view, they should be issued within 48 hours of the board meeting. This will ensure the directors accurately remember what happened during the meeting. Normally the chair will approve a draft of the minutes and circulate it to all of the board members. They will then have to agree within a day or two. At the following board meeting, one of the items of business will be to approve the minutes of the last meeting.

The sequential process in organising a board meeting begins with the chair and the chief executive officer meeting to discuss the agenda for the next meeting. Some of the items will be permanent standing issues, while others might relate to particular issues of immediate importance. Once the draft agenda is finalised, the company secretary will issue the agenda to all the directors. This usually occurs a week or so before the meeting, allowing enough time for the members to read it. A board "pack" — including the agenda and other reports and documents — is issued and should be read before the meeting. The pack might include a report from the chief executive on the previous month's operations. The pack should always contain full financial reports, including a profit-and-loss statement, a balance sheet, a cashflow statement and, in my view, a cashflow forecast. The papers might include other departmental operational reports and documents with specific proposals requiring board approval. It might be useful to mark some board papers *for decision,* while others might be marked *for information only,* as they need only to be read by the directors.

A director is to attend the board meetings having read the board papers. I recommend putting all board meetings for the 12 months ahead into a diary. Directors are welcome to ring the chief executive or other officers if they have any questions or need clarification on anything they've read. At the meeting the chair will declare the meeting open and deal with the agenda, item by item. As each subject is brought to the board's attention, directors should be invited to provide their own comments on the topic, or better still, ask questions if they wish to challenge any points of view. Collectively, the board will form a view on a decision, and once the chair is satisfied the board has reached a majority view, they will propose a motion and the board will vote by either a show of hands or general acceptance. This is then recorded in the minutes as a decision of the board. Any director can ask that a vote by them to the contrary be recorded. The chair will conclude the meeting and advise the date of the next one and inform the directors that the minutes will be issued for correction and approval in the next few days.

I keep referring to monthly board meetings as this is the most common practice; however, some boards only meet every two or three months. In fact, the minimum requirement is for only one meeting a year, where the board must approve the annual audited accounts and elect new directors. But what happens if the company requires the board to make an urgent decision between meetings? The law allows for a circulating resolution, generally called a "flying minute". In this case, the company secretary will issue a paper to all directors, usually by email, with a particular motion seeking a yes or no answer. Once the company secretary has collected the votes electronically, the decision is either approved or not for immediate implementation or action. It is important the board ratifies this decision at its next meeting so it's recorded in the minutes. Once the minutes are approved at the following board meeting, the chair will sign them, and they become the official record of that meeting and cannot be changed. Quite often courts will use the minutes of board meetings as evidence to help them determine the decision of the board and what action was taken in making that decision.

If you do find yourself ending up as a director on a board, I recommend you consider your role as more than just having to attend the board meetings. You should become involved in the company, but not involved in operations. There's an old saying, *nose in and hands out*. I tend to use the phrase that directors need to stay out of the kitchen. In other words, don't get involved in operational matters, no matter how much you think you're trying to help. The best ways a director can be more active is to attend company functions, visit operational sites, meet the staff and do further reading on the industry the company operates within, broadening their knowledge and understanding.

When a director joins a board, they should be given an induction by the chair, although this doesn't always happen. A proper induction allows a new director to gain an understanding from the chair of past issues and how the board operates. A new director should also meet the senior executives of the company and be given access to any information that will help deepen their understanding of operations. A director has the legal right to ask for any information about the company.

In my experience, new board members often sit quietly through their first board meeting, listening to the others. They might be required to vote, but I believe it's wise to absorb the whole culture of the board before becoming more active. In saying this, the sooner a director starts contributing the better. By asking questions or offering opinions or ideas, the more value a director has as a board member. I have also been involved with boards where some people talk too much while others don't say anything. A good chair should encourage quiet people to express their views so the whole board has the value of different perspectives before making a decision.

Should you find yourself with a position as a director on a board, you will encounter the concept of corporate governance. What is corporate governance? In many books, it is defined as the systems and procedures used in governing a corporation. This might not provide much help to you, and I will discuss this in greater detail in the next chapter, but essentially, it is the process where the board of directors governs the company in the interest of the shareholders and other stakeholders. Corporate governance is not the management of the company; that is the role of the executives whose job it is to implement decisions made by the board.

The role of the board and a director, in a commercial setting, is to help the company achieve profits in order to pay dividends to shareholders. But, as discussed earlier, if the organisation is a company limited by guarantee, those profits must be retained by the company to be used in furthering its objectives. If a director is appointed to a government board by a Commonwealth or state minister, the company will be owned by the respective government and that shareholding minister, and it might have its own set of rules about how the board operates. It could be that the statutory authority or government company is there to provide a service to the community, rather than make a profit. In this instance, a director needs to understand what the aims of such a company are if they're appointed to one of these boards.

In the case of family companies, most of the board will be family members, and the company's aim will be to make profits for distribution to family members. Often a non-family member is invited to such a board to bring a fresh view to the strategic growth and standards of corporate governance in that company.

In summary, the role of a director on a board is important and should be taken seriously. A director should always strive to ask questions, seek more information and read all board papers. Where no conflict of interest exists, they should participate fully in all board decisions. While a non-executive director is often only a part-time role, their liability exists 365 days a year.

Chapter 4:
Functions of a Board

f you Google "Tricker Model" you will see an interesting matrix about what a board should do. This model talks about internal accountability as well as external accountability, whereas the other part of the matrix talks about monitoring and performance. What the model says is you need to monitor the internal workings of the company (such as financial reports), while providing accountability to external regulators (such as audited tax returns and so on).

The monitoring role of a board means keeping an eye on everything within the company through the reports the board receives to see if there are any trends or issues emerging. The performance part of the company talks about setting policies and reviewing strategy for the future. In other words, the board provides oversight and foresight. In fact, the four functions of a board are primarily:

1. Strategy

2. Monitoring

3. Risk management

4. CEO's role

Strategy involves the foresight mentioned above. Here the board and senior management look to the future to ensure the company's longer-term goals (3–5 years) are on track and achievable. And ask questions like what has changed in the outside business environment that might impact on the company?

Monitoring relates to the role of oversight, reviewing all aspects of the company by way of monthly reports from management. This should cover such things as detailed finances, risk management changes, HR or people issues, marketing reports, legal and compliance matters, and any other aspect of the business to be monitored.

Risk management is a critical part of the board's role when acting on behalf of shareholders and relates to watching how the company manages any risks. This might include separate risk management sessions outside of the board meetings, regular risk identification and ranking, and considering what steps have been taken to reduce such risks.

The CEO role includes the board being involved in recruiting a new CEO and deciding when they should leave the company. It also involves a robust annual performance review of the CEO, as well as professional development and the remuneration they receive. The chair is the key contact with the CEO on behalf of the whole board.

If a board effectively deals with these four functions, it's probably doing a pretty good job. However, in my experience, strategy often gets overlooked and neglected. If a board puts strategy as the first item on the agenda after the official opening proceedings it allows the directors to spend more time looking at the company's future, rather than simply spending most of the meeting looking at the past, such as last month's results.

Quite often a board will have a separate strategy day once a year where senior executives and the board will meet to plan the next three or four years and make changes to what it's doing in order to achieve its objectives. A board also may have a separate risk management day where it focuses on the risks that are captured in the risk framework, and it analyses what steps are being taken to reduce any risks that might damage the company.

It's quite common for the chief executive to sit through the whole board meeting in order to answer any questions and comment on the written reports. It is also good practice to invite the chief financial officer to attend the board meeting for discussions about the financial reports. This is again to answer any questions and provide comments about the financial health of the company.

The board might occasionally decide to invite other members of staff who have a particular skill or area of specialty that the board would like to know more about. It is also not uncommon for a board to invite an outside person to attend a board meeting as a guest speaker on a particular topic. In all of this, the chair is the key person in controlling the time, so the board meeting is completed in a reasonable duration without dragging on too long.

The board will also receive reports and recommendations from its various committees, from which it will make decisions. The board should spend time planning its own activities, including agreeing on a board calendar for the next 12 months. Most committees meet only two or three times a year. The calendar might also include a strategy day, a risk management day and any other activity the board decides are necessary.

The other part of the board's role is to monitor its own performance. It often surprises me how often boards do a performance review on the chief executive officer but not on themselves. Whether directors do this internally or invite an external consultant to do a review is up to the board. Either way, it's important for the chair to manage the process so that the board is aware of any shortcomings or inefficiencies in how it operates and that it takes steps to correct them.

I also suggest the board puts aside some funds in its budget for the professional development of all board members. Generally, the chair will manage this process and will recommend courses or other readings to individual directors that will improve their ability to contribute.

Of course, if it is a publicly listed company on the Australian Securities Exchange, the board will have an annual general meeting and all shareholders will be invited to attend. In recent times we have seen an increase in activism by shareholders not satisfied that the company is operating in their interests. However, the shareholders have limited rights. They can only approve the appointment or re-election of directors and vote on the remuneration arrangements, as indicated earlier. (This is a nonbinding vote on the board.)

It is likely the board will enjoy some social time together, such as a meal or drink after a board meeting. This is good as it builds team spirit among the board members, and they will get to know their fellow directors better. The problem is sometimes some individuals exhibit behaviour that is not conducive to a team effort. The chair is responsible for dealing with this. I'll talk more about this in the next chapter.

Chapter 5:
Board Problems

As I mentioned in the previous chapter, there will be times when an individual director can cause problems for the whole board. This might be for a number of reasons. A director might become too involved in operations and try to give instructions to staff. They might disrupt board meetings by dominating the discussions and not allowing others to have their say. Equally, they might sit through board meetings silently without contributing. In these circumstances, it is the chair's role to have a private conversation with that person to advise them such behaviour is not acceptable. The chair should provide advice on how they can change.

A board cannot remove a director; this is entirely

up to the shareholders or members. When someone is appointed to a government or commercial board, they might not know all the directors and they might encounter individuals who are difficult to work with. It's important for a director to retain independent views when voting on board decisions, but at the same time contribute to a collegiate atmosphere so the team can work smoothly in providing the highest standards of corporate governance.

There are also times when the chief executive is the problem and refuses to cooperate with the board. This is easily fixed. A board has the authority in its constitution to remove or terminate a chief executive at any time and appoint a new one. In the case of family companies, the founder is often the major shareholder and tends to have dominance over the board and often will remove or appoint directors on their own.

In the case of government boards, only the minister can appoint or remove directors, and it is the responsibility of the board to deal with any bad behaviour. The best course of action here is for the chair to meet with the shareholding minister and advise them that one individual director is causing major disruptions. This allows the minister to decide on their removal.

Other problems a board might encounter can occur when the company faces a major crisis. This might be the death of an employee at a work site, a sudden economic downturn or a global event such as a pandemic. Such situations might require the board to act urgently, and it is not uncommon for a board to have a telephone or video meeting outside of regular business hours to discuss the crisis and decide what action needs to be taken to protect the company. Any decisions made must result in a flying minute, which then needs to be recorded and ratified at the next board meeting. A crisis might also require directors to travel to another location to see the issues for themselves and make decisions quickly. When a crisis occurs, it's essential that a board has two important documents in place. The first is a disaster action plan. This should outline the different responsibilities of the board and the executive when taking action to resolve the disaster or crisis. This will allow the board to quickly implement protocols in a crisis. The second is a business recovery plan which will help the company to rebuild after a crisis.

Obviously, workplace health and safety is important in any company, but should an accident or fatality occur on a work site, the board needs to respond quickly. In recent times, the Commonwealth and states have introduced industrial manslaughter legislation, which effectively means directors will be held liable for the death of an employee unless it can be proved the company had appropriate systems in place to avoid such events.

The other problem I have seen over the years that can affect boards is complacency. If a board consists of the same people over many years, directors almost unintentionally form a club, and they agree to agree on everything. They can form the attitude that if it's not broken, don't fix it. And that if nothing has happened in the past, then it probably won't happen in the future. Of course, this is the wrong attitude, and a healthy board should have robust discussions and disagreements from time to time in order to stay up to date and relevant. For a director to contribute meaningfully to such a robust discussion, they should form an independent view and challenge the status quo if it's necessary to make the rest of the board aware of issues they might have fallen asleep at the wheel on.

This brings me to the point about board renewal. In the case of companies listed on the stock exchange, directors are re-elected by the shareholders at each annual general meeting. However, in practice, they tend to stay in the role and are often re-elected for many years. Generally, after five or six years, if a director hasn't either developed the skills or desire to be nominated as the chair, they should consider leaving the board to allow a new face at the board table. I once met a chairman who had been 28 years in that role and was very proud of it. As I told him, that's probably 20 years too long. Generally, the chair should think about finding a replacement for themselves after 10 years or so. In some instances, the constitution might dictate such a requirement. Regardless, a board should discuss succession planning, and this should be done through its remunerations and nominations committee.

One of the other problems a board might encounter is not having the skills needed to deal with specific problems. For this reason, I always recommend a board undertake a skills gap analysis to identify what skills they are lacking, especially in areas of particular need for their company. These might include strategic thinking, human resources, information technology, marketing, finance analysis and legal knowledge. Once a board has identified gaps in members' skills, it should then seek out people with those skills to be available for appointment or election at the next annual general meeting.

Chapter 6:
Boards and Technology

Often by the time people have gained enough experience to be appointed to a board, they have started to grow a few grey hairs! Although not necessarily so, a board comprised of older members might have less insight into the rapidly changing world of technology and how it impacts the company. For this reason, a board might benefit from having either a younger board member or one with up-to-date specialist knowledge of IT and social media.

Recent surveys have found one of the biggest challenges for a board is hacking or cyber-attacks — where outside parties attempt to infiltrate IT systems and gain access to such information as financial records, staff records, customer records or other vital information. It is important that board members understand how capable the company's systems are at protecting against hacking attempts.

Board members should also be aware of the latest trends in technology that might allow the company to grow faster and ultimately offer better returns to shareholders. In the event directors don't fully understand the latest technology, I recommend establishing an IT committee and bringing in outside expertise to make recommendations to the board.

I have seen companies forced to close because their competitors have surpassed them in their use of the latest technology which the board of the old company failed to consider or invest in. Other companies have used cutting-edge technology to gain a competitive advantage in the marketplace. On that note, social media appears to be the strongest marketing trend for companies today. And it might be the case that traditional avenues of advertising, such as newspapers, magazines or other media, are not only expensive, but they might fail to reach the target audience or customers. It's important that directors understand the power of social media and how it can be used for the benefit of the company. However, all of this needs to be considered in light of privacy legislation, where the board has the responsibility to ensure the privacy of its staff, customers and suppliers.

For this reason, a good board will be familiar with the *Privacy Act 1988*, and in particular, the *Privacy Amendment (Notifiable Data Breaches) Act 2017*. This legislation, introduced in 1998, requires a company to advise the government if a data breach of any of its records occurs. A data breach can happen both as a result of human error within the company or as an external malicious attack. Companies with a turnover of less than $3 million a year are not required to comply with the *Privacy Act 1988*. It's also useful for a director to compare the privacy policies of other publicly listed companies with their own. Not only will this help them understand how other companies operate when it comes to privacy, it will help directors check how robust the privacy principles are within their own company.

Boards are increasingly using technology to operate more efficiently, including software systems or portals that allow directors to securely access all required board records through their computer or tablet. The *Corporations Act 2001* has been amended to allow for the electronic transfer of such records or information, including board decisions by flying minute. Another issue for directors who are not IT savvy might occur when they are presented with a decision to approve expenditure on large software platforms, networks or hardware decisions that often involve large amounts of money. If necessary, the board might need to get independent advice from IT specialists to review any such proposal. The board might want to engage an independent organisation to monitor the installation of the project to ensure it is delivered on time and within budget, over and above the management reports they get. It should be in a language the board understands without all the technical acronyms and jargon. A good board will embrace technology and invest in it to grow the company.

Chapter 7:
Before you join a Board

Many potential directors think about joining a board without reflecting on the risk of personal financial liability or reputational damage. And often without properly investigating the company and the people in it. Often directors have told me that if they'd known what they were letting themselves in for they might have had second thoughts. The trouble is it's too late by then. And as I discussed earlier, a director's liability starts from the moment they are legally recorded as a director. For this reason, if you're ever invited to become part of a board, it's important to undertake due diligence on the company before accepting the position and signing the consent to act as a director. This includes asking for a lot of company information (on a confidential basis) as part of your research. You can find much information about a company and its past through Google. However, you should ask to see the last two or three board packs and minutes and find out such information as where and when the meetings will be held.

I also advise reading the company's constitution and strategic plan. Before you accept you should also ask to meet not only the chair but some of the other directors, and indeed, the chief executive officer and other senior managers. When you meet with these people, ask them if they have a risk management process in place and whether any adverse risk incidents have occurred in the past. You should also ask if there is any legal action being taken against the company — or if the company itself has taken legal action against others. It is worth checking if there is any evidence of legal action in recent years.

It is essential to look at the financial affairs of the company to see how financially healthy it is. And, in particular, how solvent it is. You might meet the chief financial officer to get their view on the finances of the company, both now and looking forward. It's too late once you're appointed to the board to find out that for some years the company has been going backward financially. Because when crunch time comes, your liability will start.

It is wise to ask yourself if the company is a place that suits your interests and skills, and if your particular skills and experience will assist in the company furthering its objectives. Will you be allowed to make a meaningful contribution? How independent will you be allowed to be on the board? How much will you be expected to toe the line rather than form your own view? You want to clearly understand what's expected of you as a board or committee member. And obviously, you might want to ask about the remuneration arrangements and reimbursement of expenses. I have seen cases where a potential director has been allowed to sit through a board meeting so they can see the board in action before they accept the offer. However, this might not always be allowed. You might ask for a copy of your letter of appointment so you can see clearly all the matters that are important to you.

Finally, ask yourself, how well will you fit with these people around the board table? Do you want your name associated with this company? Can you add value to the board? Will you have the time and energy to fulfil your duties and responsibilities? Do you have any conflicts of interest? And importantly, would you, as a shareholder, put your money into this company? And if not, why?

If any of this due diligence causes you concern, you need to think carefully before allowing flattery to overtake reality. While it's nice to be invited to join a board, you need to be aware of what you're getting into once you are a director. Of course, you might think that if you're not happy, you can resign not long after you start, but that's not going to do your reputation much good as people will know that you served for only a short term, and they will want to know why. So, what's the key takeaway from this chapter? Focus on one of the important board basics, and do your homework before you join a board.

Chapter 8:
Getting on a Board

As I said in my introduction, the idea for this book came about after talking to postgraduate business students and realising that one day they might be interested in trying to obtain a board appointment as part of their professional career. Although you might not be a university student, you might have the same aspirations. And regardless, these are a few tips I would give anyone looking at getting on a board.

1. Get a career coach or business mentor to advise you

2. Keep investing a small percentage of your income in your personal and professional development

3. Develop a lifelong love of learning

4. Build a career plan with milestones as to where you want to be over the years

5. Network constantly in business circles

6. Work smarter, not harder

7. Learn to recognise opportunities before they pass you by

8. Find your purpose in life (in terms of your career)

Having said that, here are some resources you can use to find board opportunities. If you join the Australian Institute of Company Directors (www.aicd.com.au) and pay a small extra fee each year you will receive a weekly email with all the board vacancies they have listed around Australia. A lot of these are not-for-profit boards and will be voluntary, but this is a good starting point as it will help demonstrate you have some board experience when applying for other positions in the future. The Director Institute (www.directorinstitute.com.au) also provides a list of board vacancies. Another company I've found is called Board Directions (boarddirection. com.au). They charge an annual fee and you will receive a weekly list of board vacancies. Don't be surprised if you find these three sources all have a lot of the same vacancies. The state and federal governments also keep a register of potential members for its own boards, and you can send your CV for inclusion on these registers at no charge.

Networking is important because it provides an opportunity to meet existing directors or other people who are able to recognise your ability to contribute to a board, as there might be opportunities that are not advertised.

There are also many board recruitment firms operating in Australia, including major accounting firms and other individual specialists. These companies are usually paid by a client to find a suitable director to fill a vacancy and there's nothing wrong with you sending your CV with a cover letter to all of them, indicating your willingness to be considered for any future opportunities.

Having said all that, your professional skills must provide some evidence you can make a worthwhile contribution at the board level. Keep in mind the role of the board is to work on the business and not in the business, so boards are looking for strategic thinkers who can analyse risks, understand corporate finances, and can look to the future. I often say a board's role is oversight and foresight. And not just looking at the past and monitoring it, but also thinking outside the box about the future of the company.

I suggest you also need to be a good communicator — in writing and verbally. And you need to be able to quickly analyse large amounts of complex information to form an opinion before a decision is made. You also need to be an independent thinker and a team player who can get on well with your fellow board members and contribute in a meaningful way — while also accepting the majority view or decision.

Whether you want to be invited to be appointed to the board of a family company, a publicly listed company, a private company, a public unlisted company, a government board or a not-for-profit organisation, you need to be able to demonstrate in your CV that you have the skills and experience to make a useful contribution.

As I often say to people, the hardest part is getting your first board appointment. Once you have that under your belt, you'll find that the invitation for a second board appointment will come faster. And as you gain more experience, subsequent appointments tend to get even easier. Some people will join only one board in their career. And often, this will be assisting a not-for-profit organisation or because they've been invited for the specific skillset they offer. There are others, though, who make a career out of being a full-time company director. I was fortunate to reach that point where I made my living from being a company director on multiple boards, while at the same time providing corporate governance advice to other boards.

When taking a board appointment, you need to be sure you've got the time for each board. Being a director is not a hit-and-miss role. It also needs to be with a company you think you can add some value to. Or a company that you're interested in what they do and what they are trying to achieve.

Finally, develop a career plan for yourself. And good luck getting on boards in the future. The economy in Australia operates more effectively by having organisations governed by skilful and interested board members.

Chapter 9:
A Good Board

Before we finish this book, let me share with you what a good board looks like. And from that, the opposite indicates a board that is not so good.

We start with agency theory. A board of directors are "agents" of the shareholders (or members), who are the owners of the company. And it's the shareholders who vote to appoint the board and, via the constitution, give them wide-ranging powers to govern the company in shareholders' interests. In turn, the board will appoint the chief executive and assign powers to them, including the power to appoint other management and staff, and they will be expected to operate the company according to the direction of the board. Power begins with the owners and flows downwards. Poor governance is when the power flows upwards and the management starts telling a weak board what is going to happen, and that board simply rubber-stamps all such decisions. It's the board that is accountable to the owners, not management. Management is accountable to the board. A well-governed company will have a good board that understands this issue and acts accordingly.

It is important to consider what size the board should be, and the constitution will indicate the minimum and maximum size. In my experience, a board of about six or seven people will provide the range of skills needed, although a private or family company might have only three or four people. There is a lot of talk today about diversity, and it seems to focus on gender. While that is important, also consider other ways to achieve diversity, such as age, industry or other skills, ethnicity and geographic location.

A good board will have a skilled chair who can lead a group around the board table towards reaching decisions. They are the first among equals but with no further powers than any other director. They must establish a good working relationship with the CEO and all outside stakeholders. The chair also provides leadership in mentoring each board member and often will be the face of the company to the media or at company or other events. They will know all the rules of governance and ensure they are followed. They set an example of the highest integrity for the board. A good chair must be organised and decisive and be able to manage their time well. Often they will be an *ex-officio* member of all board committees, meaning they can attend any such meetings if they wish.

The directors on a good board will know their legal obligations under the *Corporations Act 2001*. These include the requirement to act in good faith at all times, the requirement to act in the best interests of the company, and the need to act with due diligence and care when making decisions. This means reading the board papers and asking questions before the meeting to ensure they are fully informed. It also means leaving mobile phones outside the meeting and listening to all the debate around the table — while asking any questions and stating their opinion without fear or favour. In the case of a charity or not-for-profit board, it means ensuring that all the requirements and regulations of the Australian Not-For-Profit and Charities Commission are followed.

An effective board will have an agenda that covers all of the important matters, without going into operations. This agenda will include financial reports, including a cashflow forecast or projection (as distinct from a cashflow statement). It also will include a report from the chief executive, as well as a report on the risk-management framework and any incidents since the last meeting. It also might include a strategy tracker to review the progress of the three-year strategic goals, and a compliance checklist to ensure the company is complying with all relevant legislation and regulations. The agenda might include other items a director would like discussed, although it's up to the chair to decide if there is time for that at the meeting. I suggest some board papers are marked "for decision" while others are marked "for information". This way only the first group are discussed and decided upon, while the last group only will be read by the directors.

A good board will have directors and officers liability insurance in place for the board members and the senior executives of the company. They will all have read the policy and understand what it covers. And more importantly, understand its exclusions and what it does *not* cover. A good board will review all the insurance for the company in its compliance checklist and risk management framework. It will have a code of conduct for the board that sets out the ethical rules in which to operate and the standards expected from all directors. A good board will have a thorough induction process for new directors under the supervision of the chair.

A good board will have a robust set of committees, each with its own charter. Each committee will have an effective chair and might include outside experts. The committees will understand that they only make recommendations to the full board, and it's the board that will make any final decision. Good board meetings will have robust debate and even disagreement at times, but once a decision is made, it is binding on all the directors. The chair should encourage all directors to have a say on each matter but bring the discussion to a decision eventually. A good board will keep accurate minutes of all meetings and ratify any flying minutes at the next formal meeting. All directors must respect the confidentiality of all board meetings. I have seen cases of directors leaking information and decisions to outside parties, including the media, and that is not acting in good faith or in the best interests of the company.

A good board will have a budget managed by the chair for ongoing professional development for all board members and the CEO. As well as the annual performance review of the CEO, the board should review its own performance each year (or every second year), either internally or by an outside consultant. A good board will probably meet in different locations depending on how widespread the company's operations are. It should certainly visit company sites to see things firsthand. All directors should attend company functions and events and not just the board or committee meetings.

A good board will agree on a set of policies that explain the operational rules for the company, and these should be well known by all staff. It will have a policy on corporate social responsibility to show its position regarding such things as the environment, the wider community, philanthropy and work practices in its supply chain. All such policies will be reviewed each year and made well known to all staff and relevant stakeholders.

A good board will have a strong succession plan in place to ensure directors know when they need to replace the chair or directors. There should be candidates already identified for such roles. The board will have a remuneration policy in place that provides an adequate reward for directors' efforts and that of the CEO but is aligned with the interests of the shareholders or members.

A good board will be well prepared for the unexpected via its risk management framework. This means having a disaster action plan for when a crisis does occur and a business recovery plan after it happens. Such a crisis might be another pandemic, a cyber-attack on its data, or a major fire that shuts down the business.

A good board will have dates for board and committee meetings on a calendar 12 months ahead, as well as days for strategic planning or risk management and the AGM. Good directors will not miss any of these meetings or events where possible.

Finally, a good board will have a clear understanding that they are the servants of the owners and will actively contribute to the growth and profitability of the company — or, in the case of a not-for-profit, the mission of the organisation. Each director will behave in a way that is respectful of the other board members and management and staff of the company, while still sharing their own views for the good of the company. A good board will function smoothly and effectively at all times and achieve its goals the company.

Summary

As I said at the outset of this book, *Board Basics* is not meant to be a technical guide to everything regarding a board of directors. It is simply an attempt to provide some of the basic information about how boards operate, and hopefully, it would have added to your own knowledge in this area. There are many resources available in the way of books, webinars, and courses –and other advisors who can fill in the details about boards. I wish you well in your search for further information.

Generally, the public thinks about boards only when something goes wrong with a company and we see it in the media. Behind the scenes there are thousands of boards operating around Australia and in other countries that ensure their company satisfies its shareholders and all of its stakeholders. In my experience, being a member of a board is very enjoyable, and I've always left a board feeling I have contributed to the benefit of that company and its owners.

Hopefully, now you have a better understanding of some of the legal structures of companies, what the role of a director is, and the functions of a board. I've also touched on some of the problems boards have to deal with and the use of technology. I've also tried to give you advice on doing due diligence before you join a board, as well as some tips on how to get on a board. Finally, I have described what a good board looks like.

Thanks for reading *Board Basics*, and I look forward to sharing further knowledge and information in the future.